This Coloring Book Belongs To

COLOR TEST PAGE

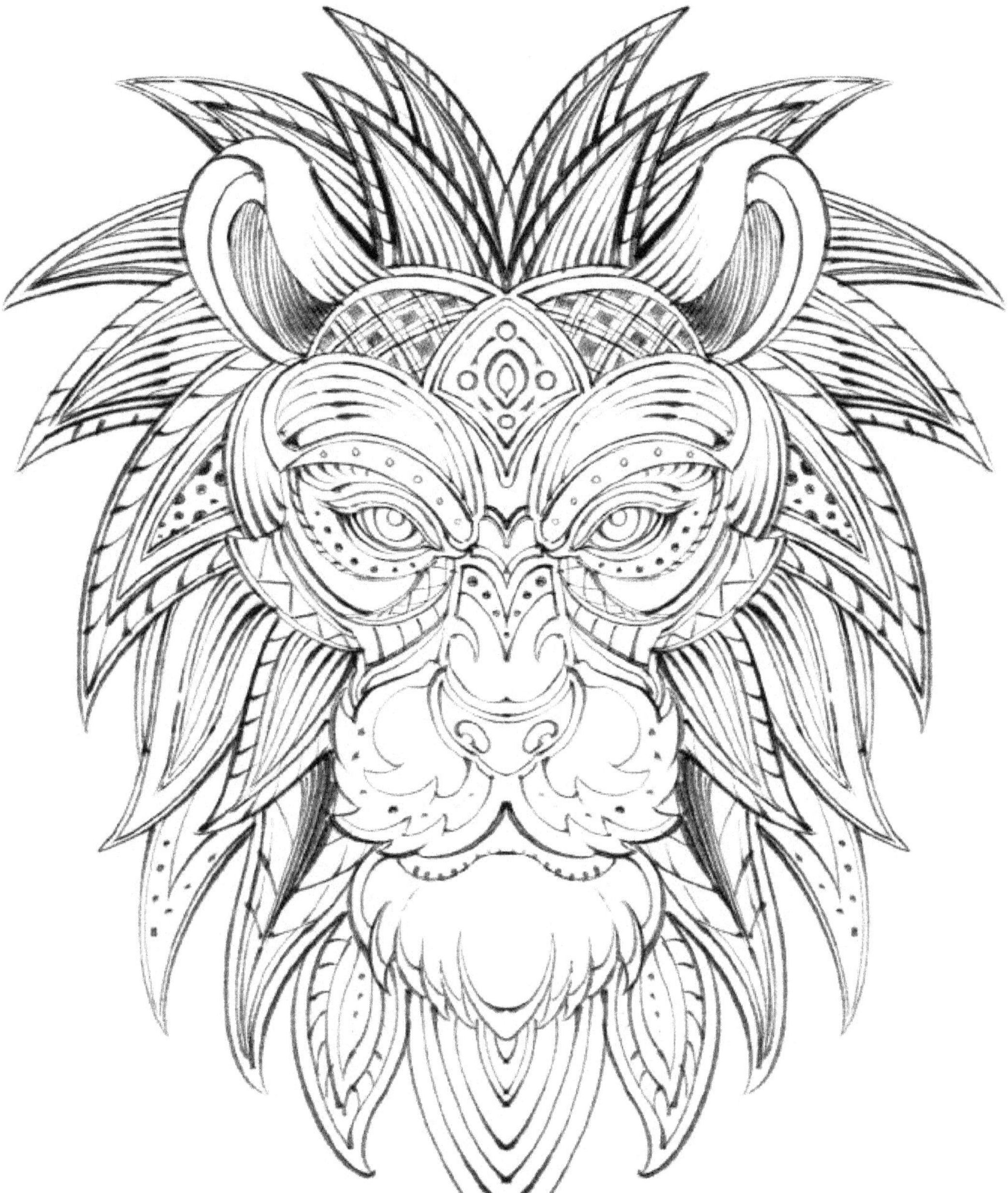

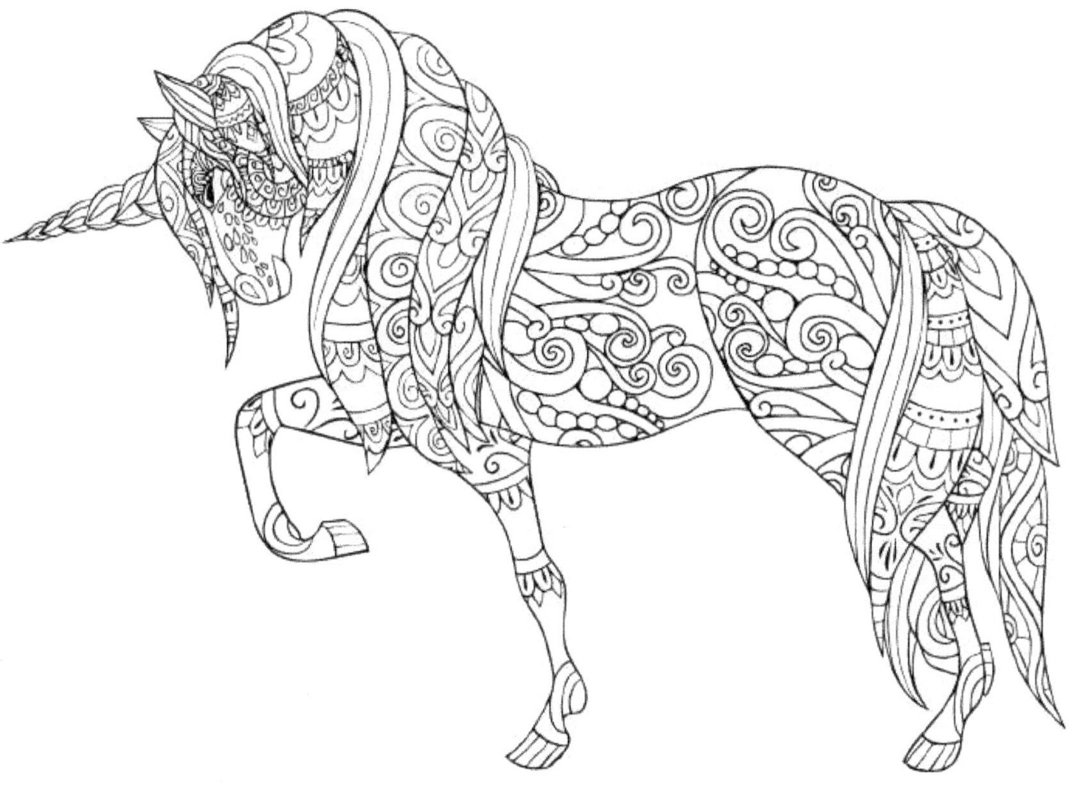

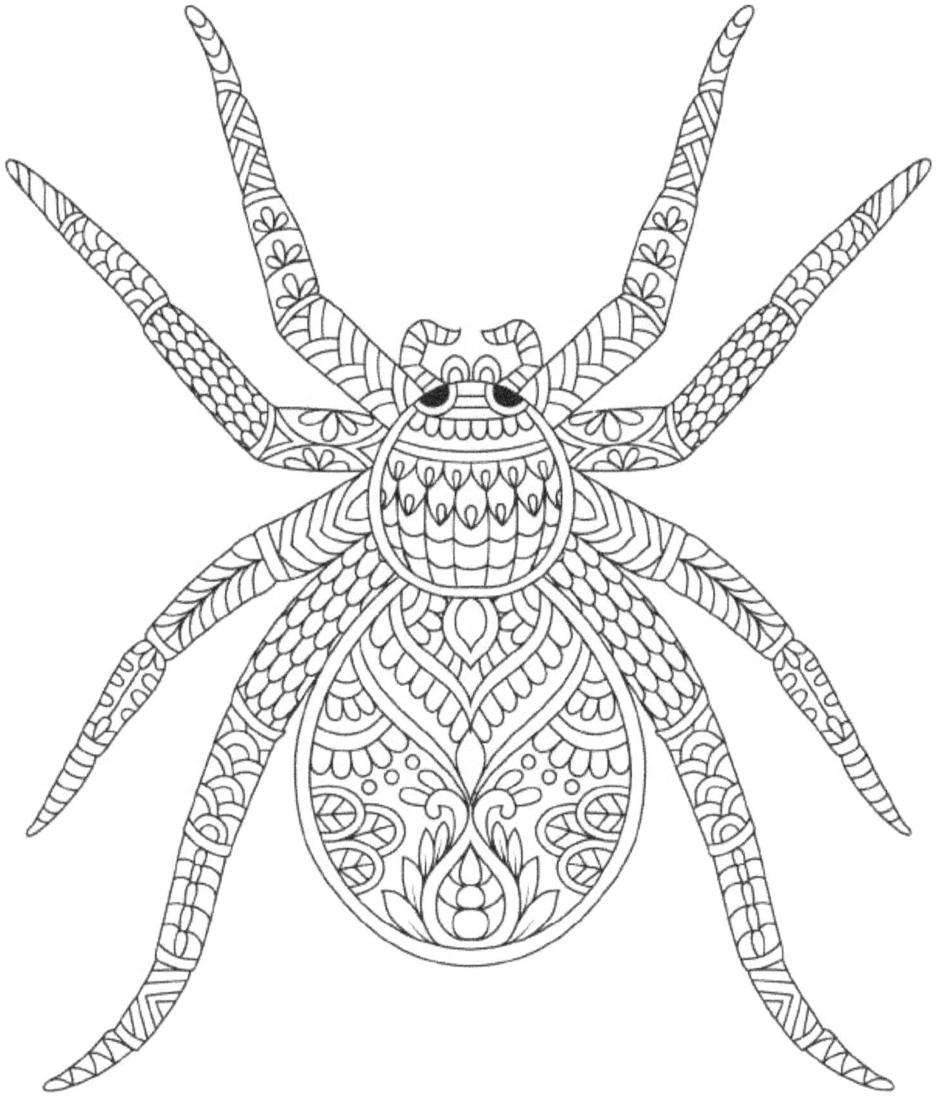

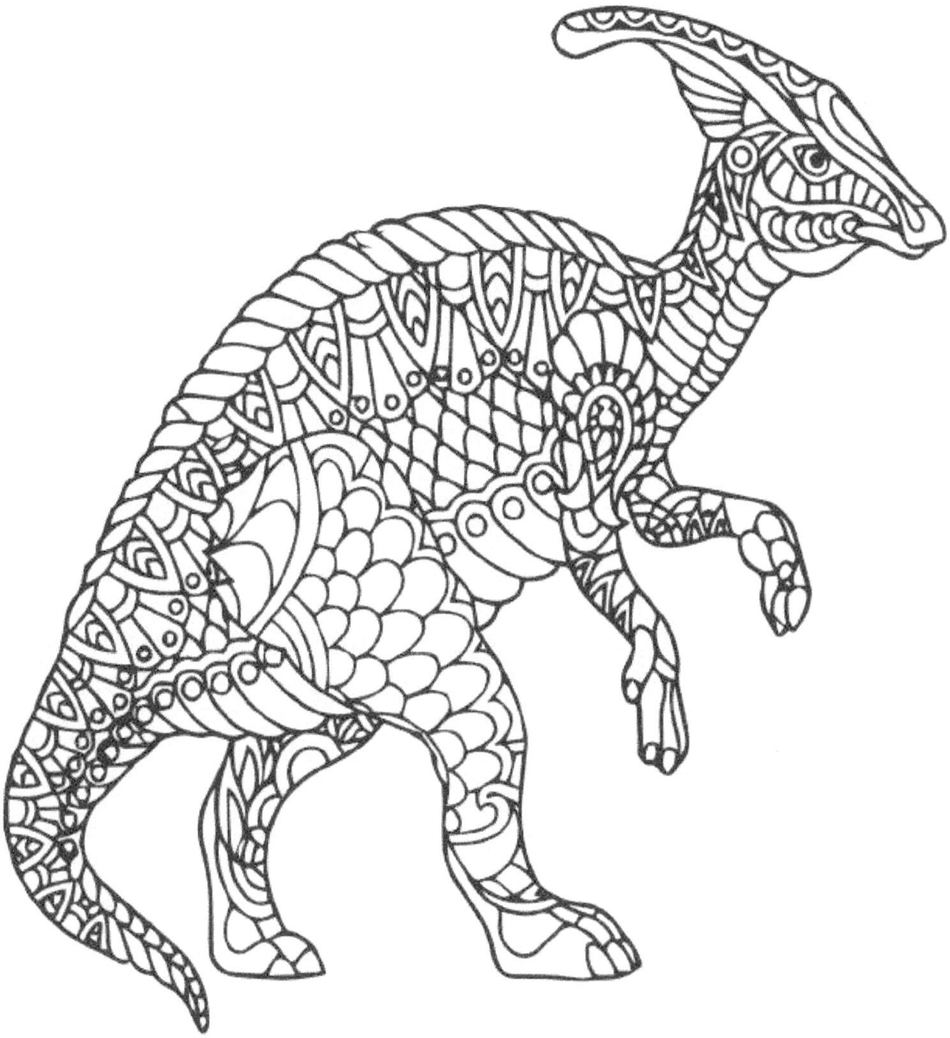

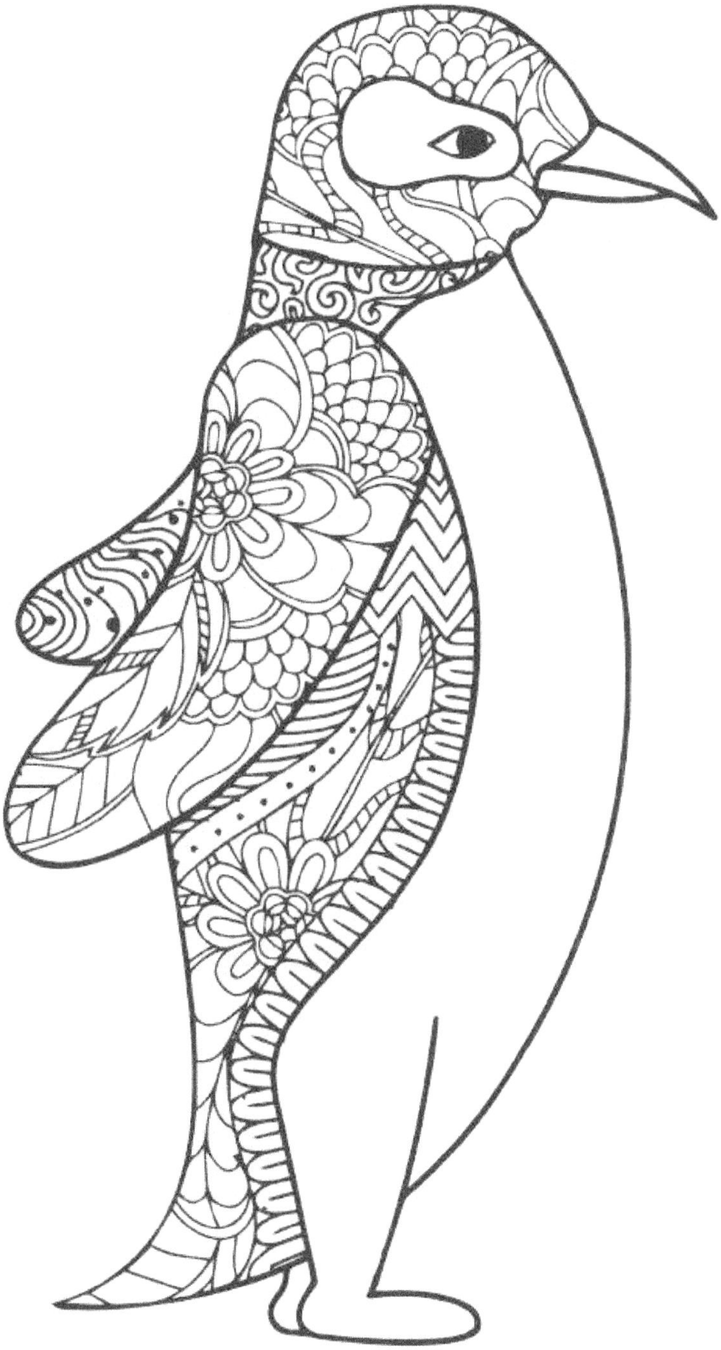

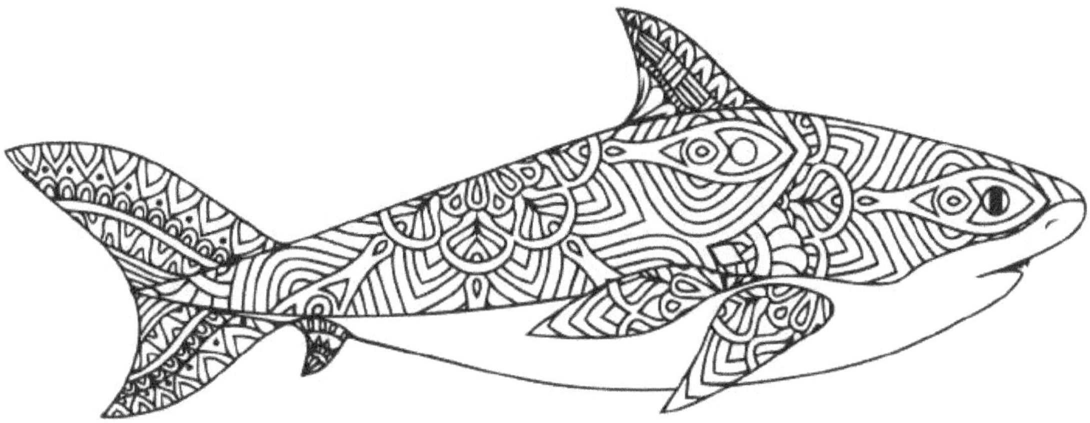

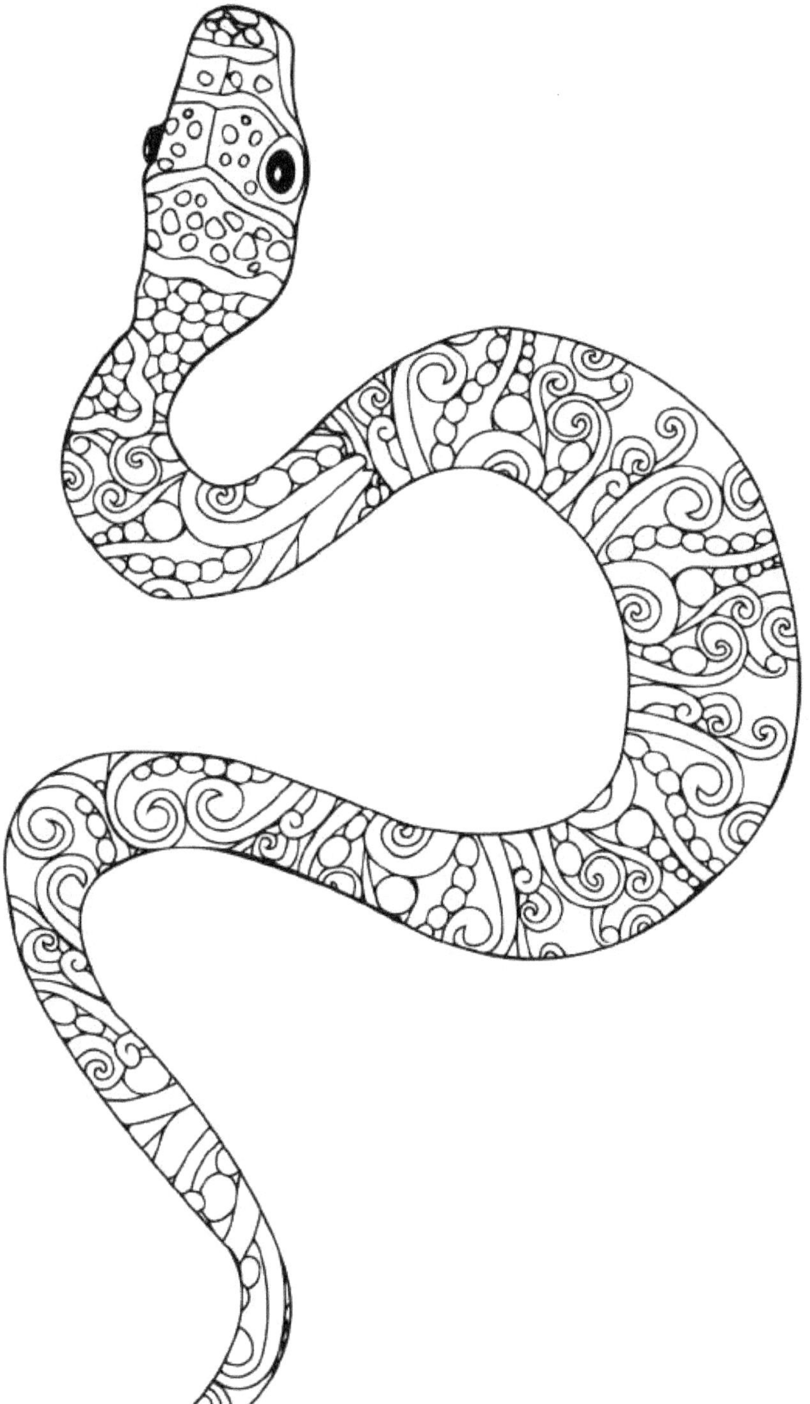

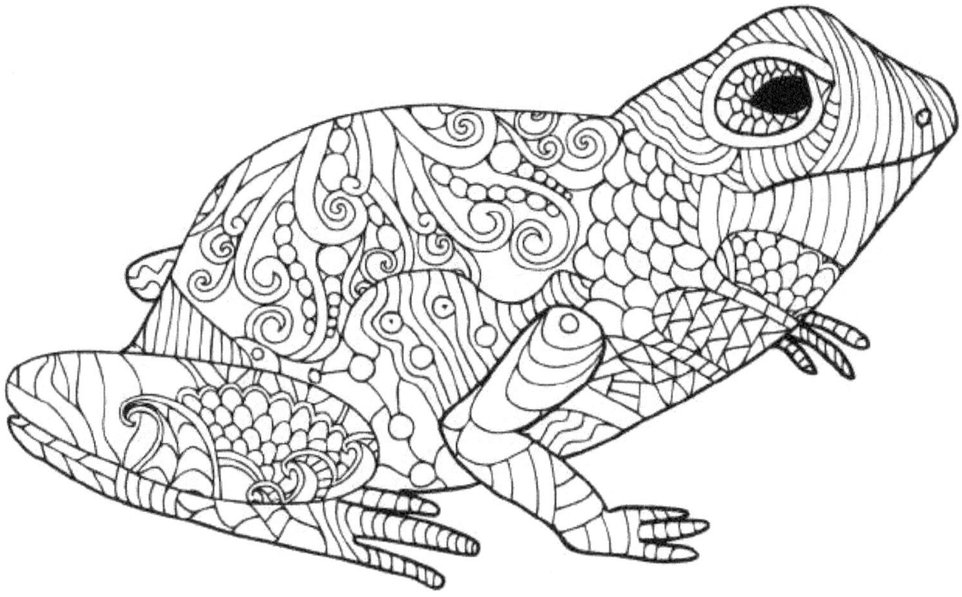

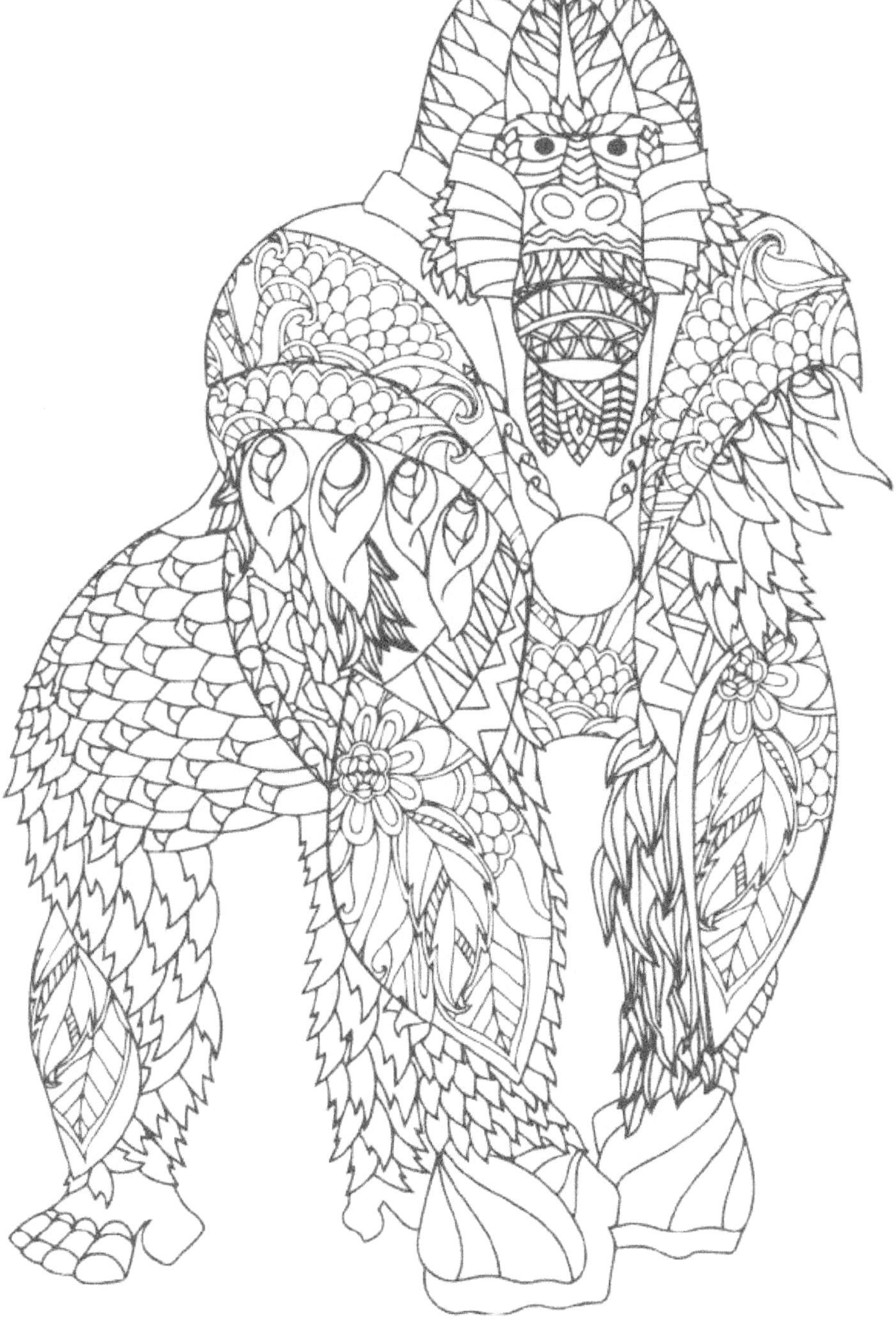

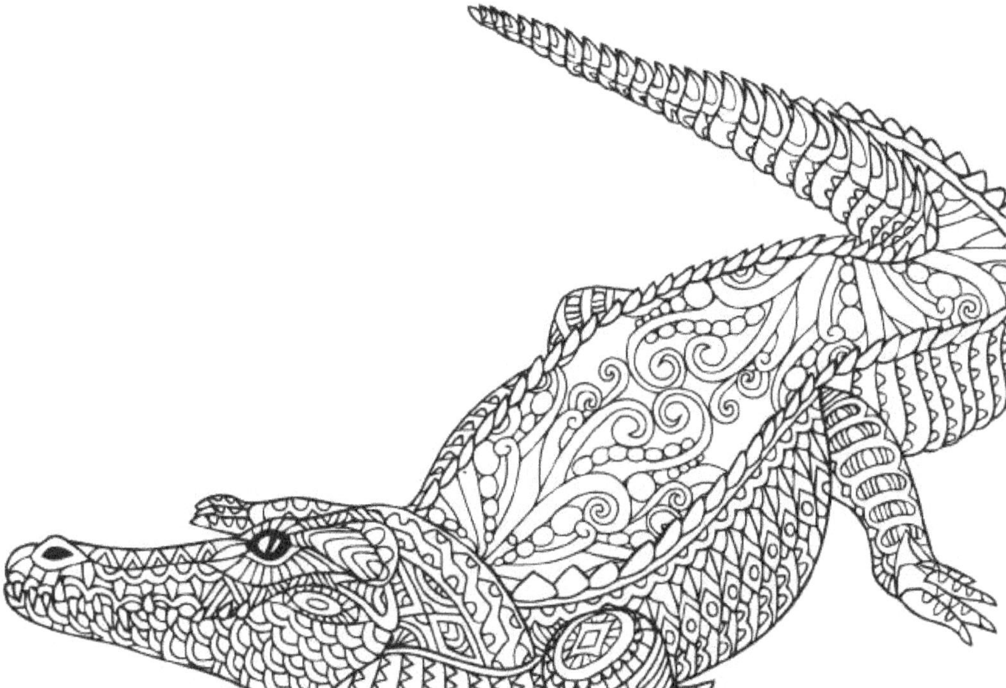

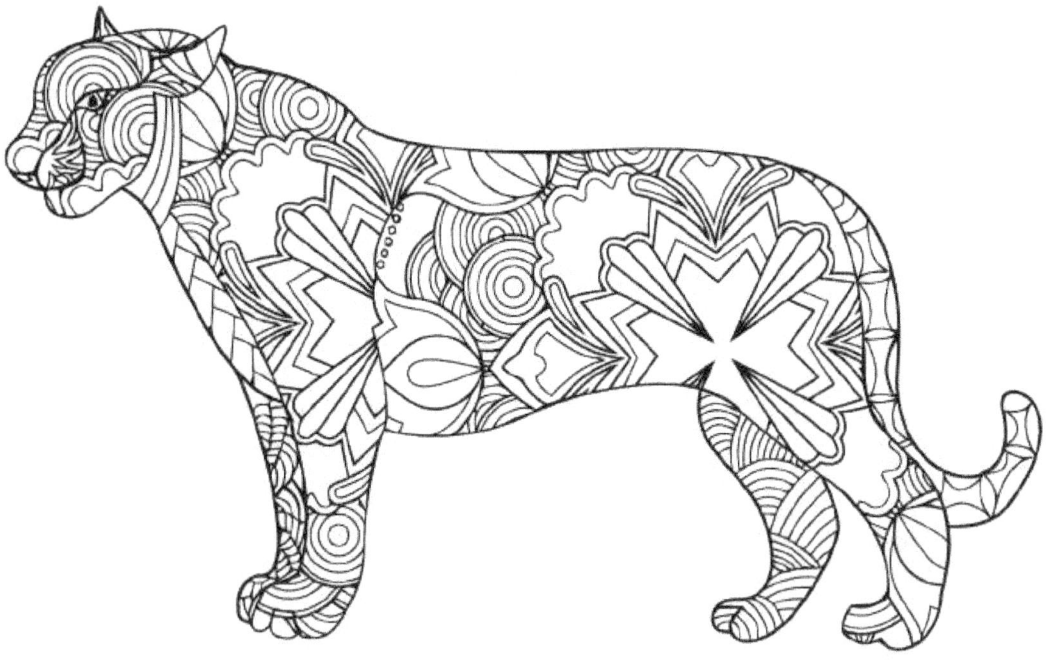

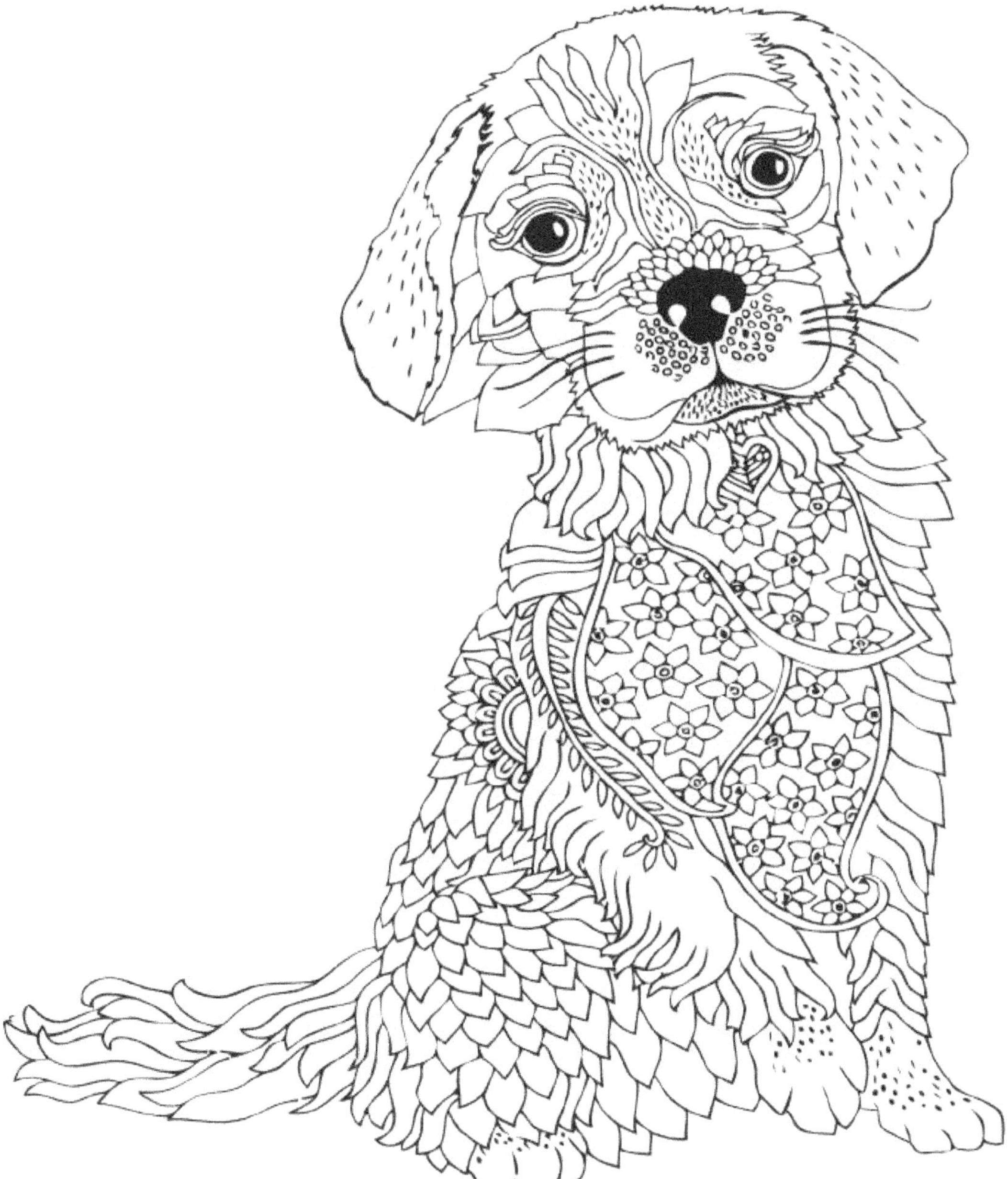

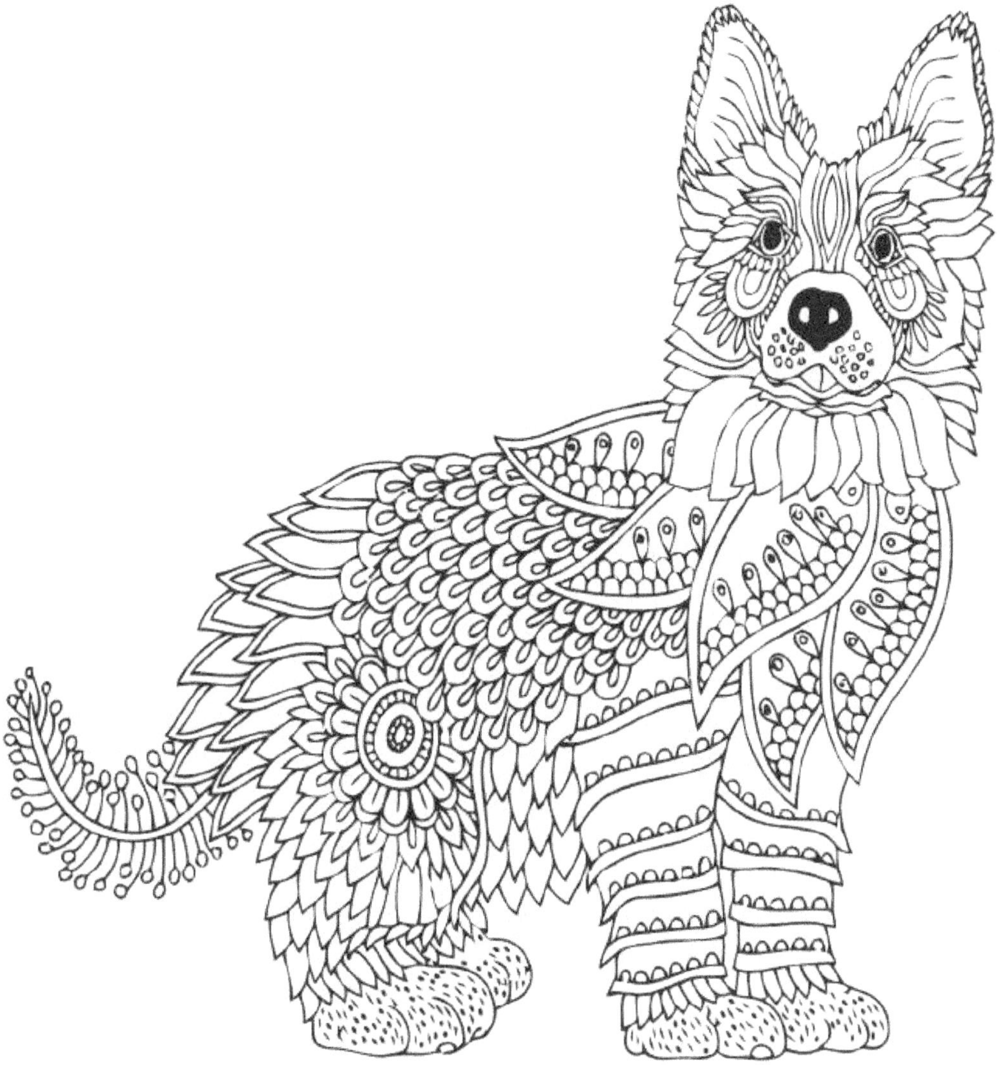

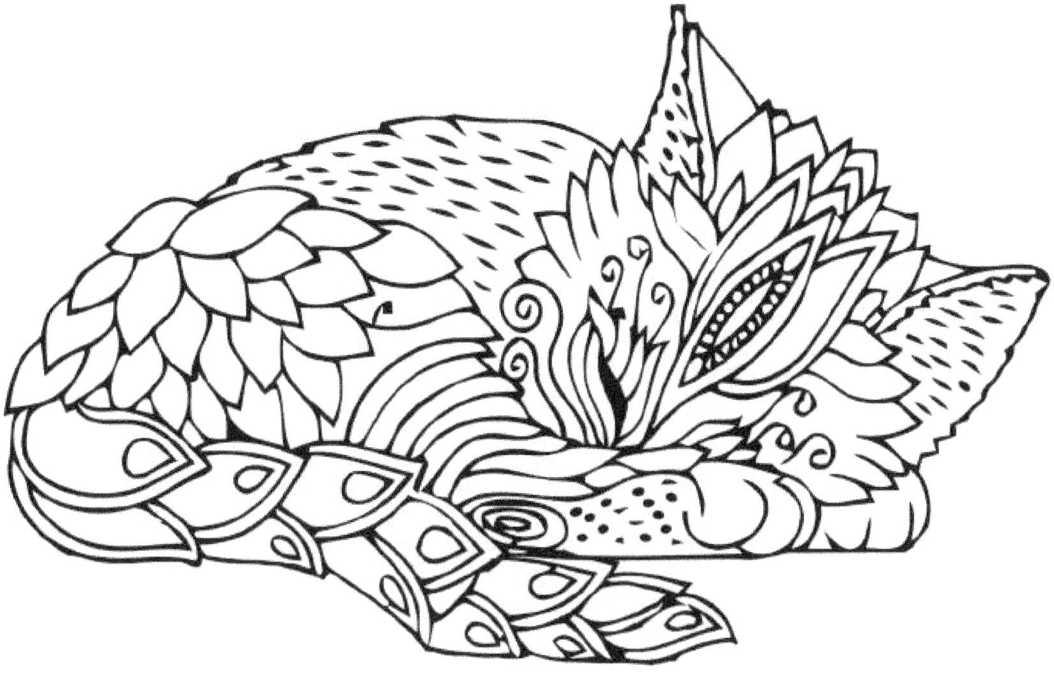

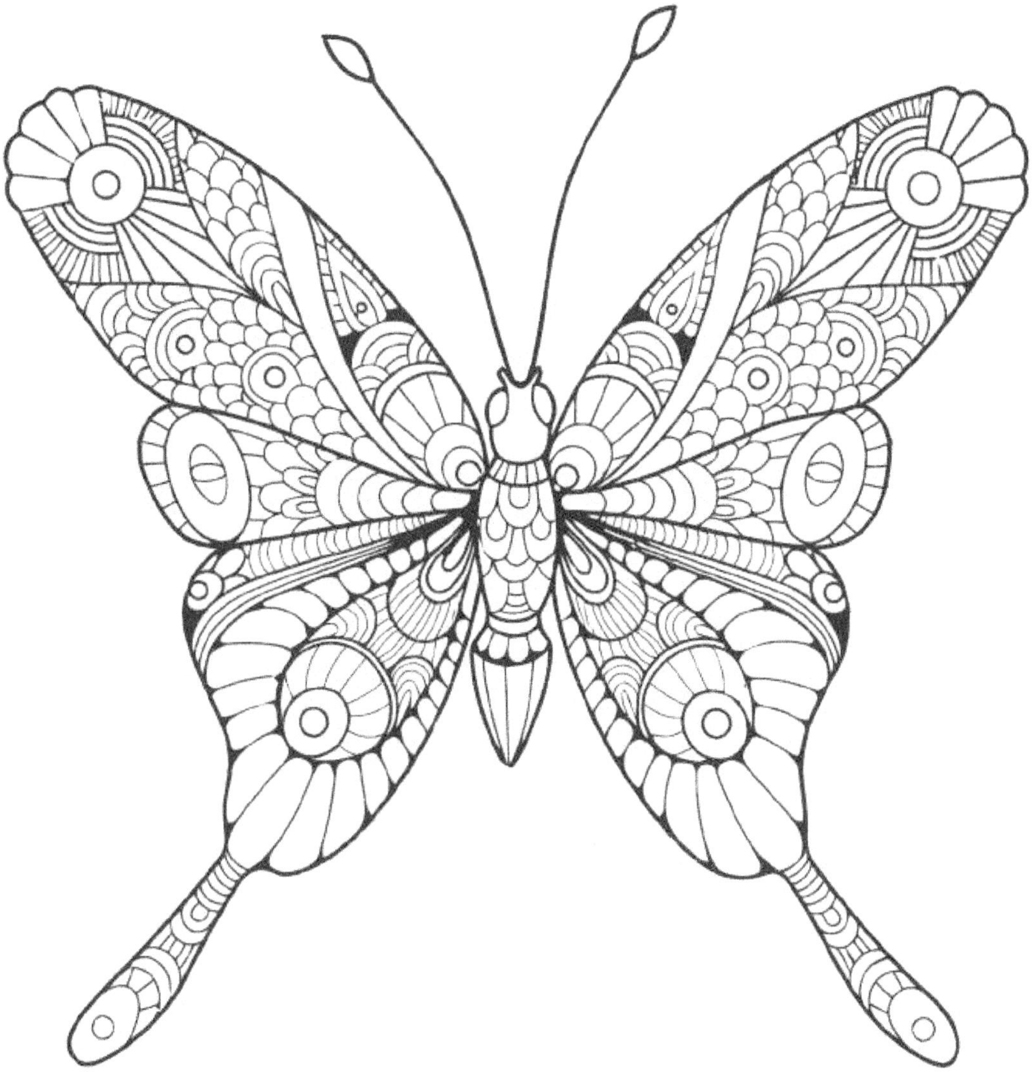

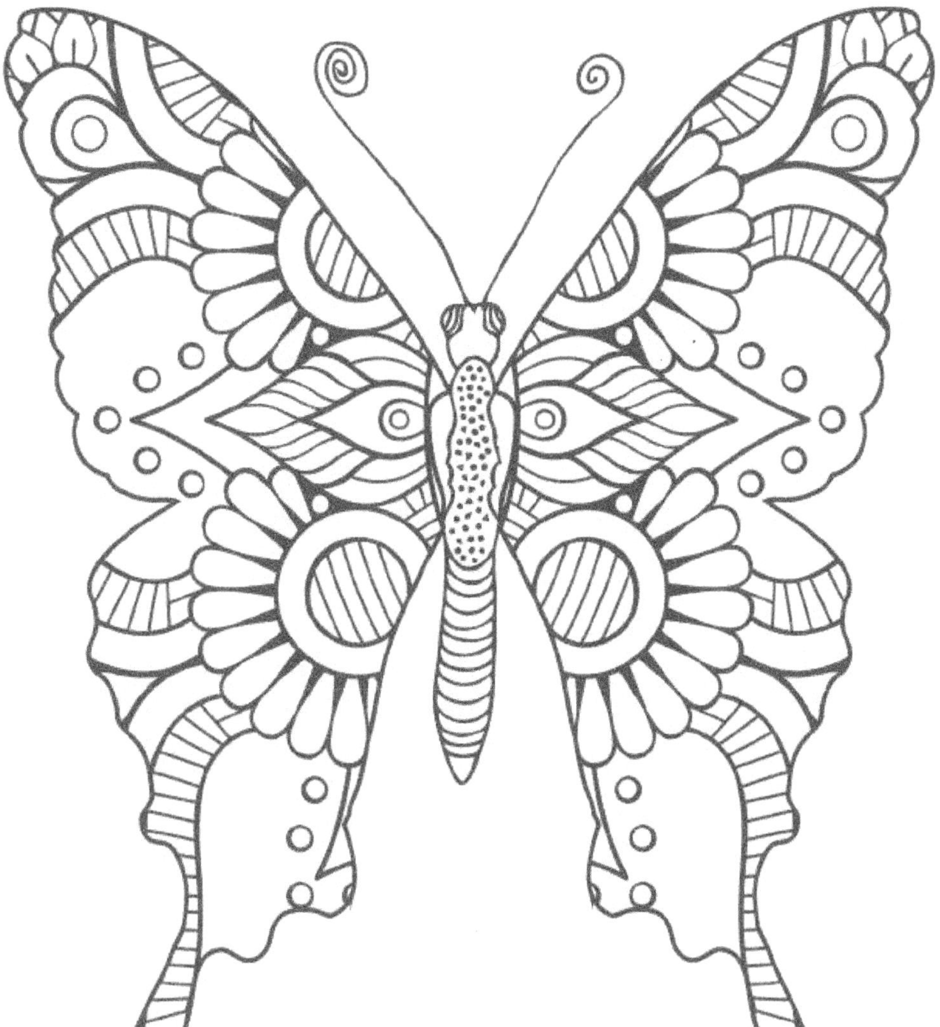

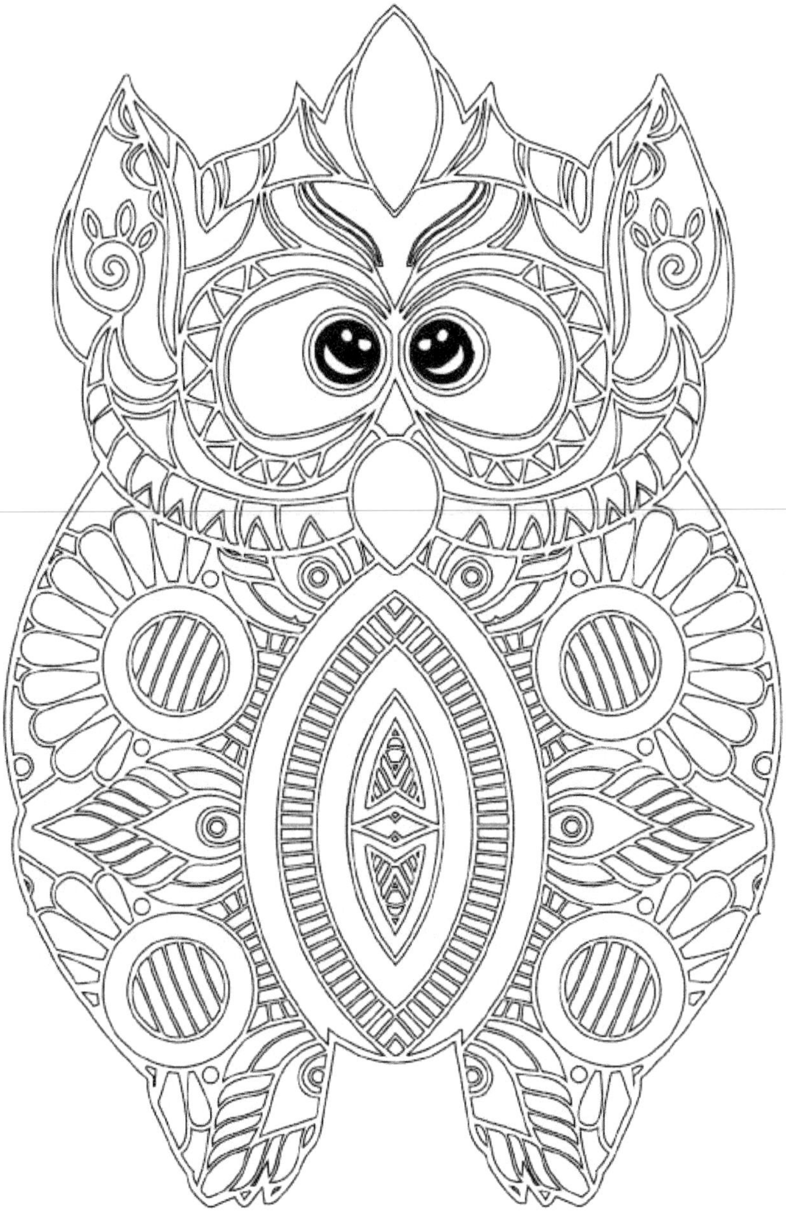

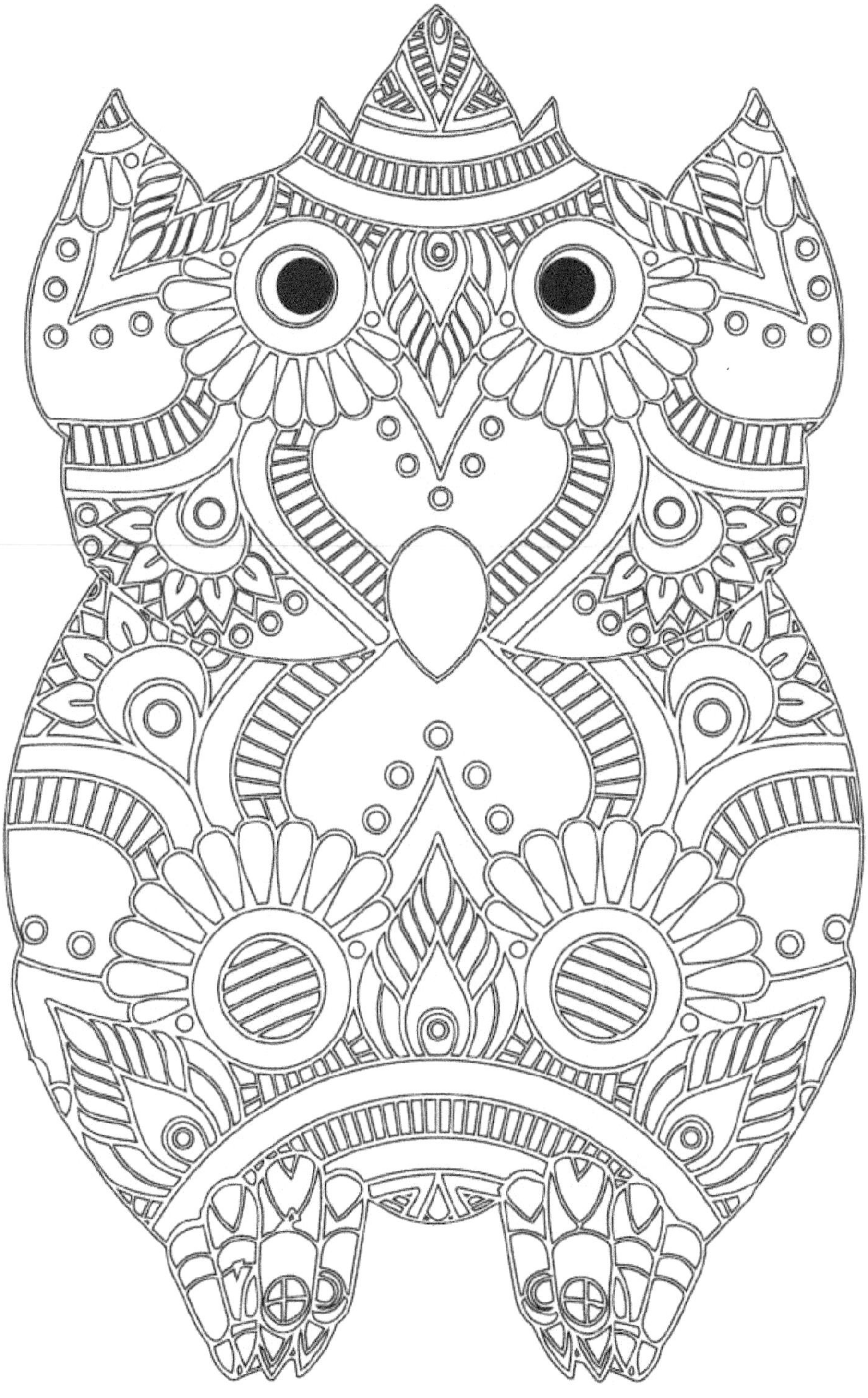

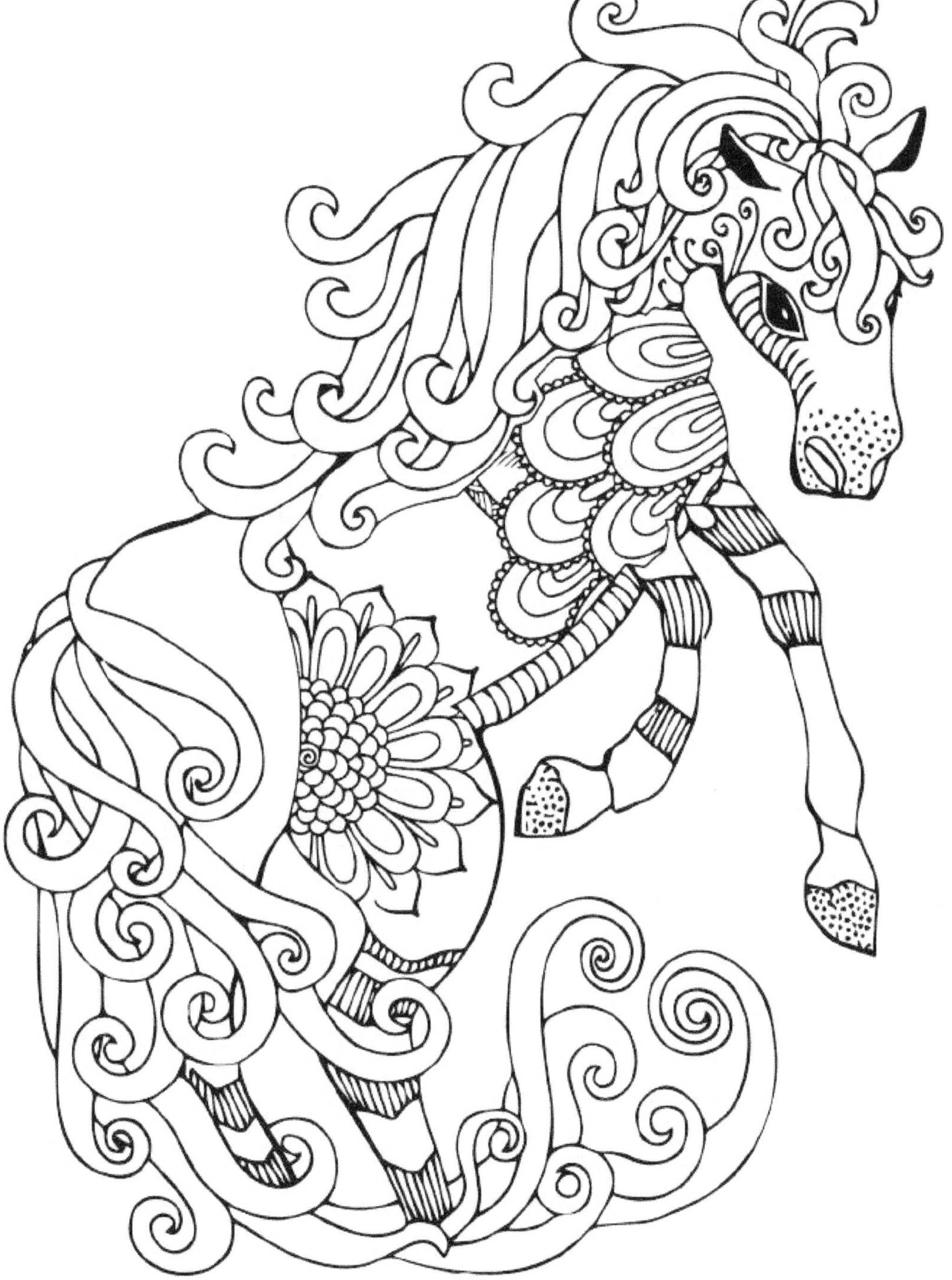

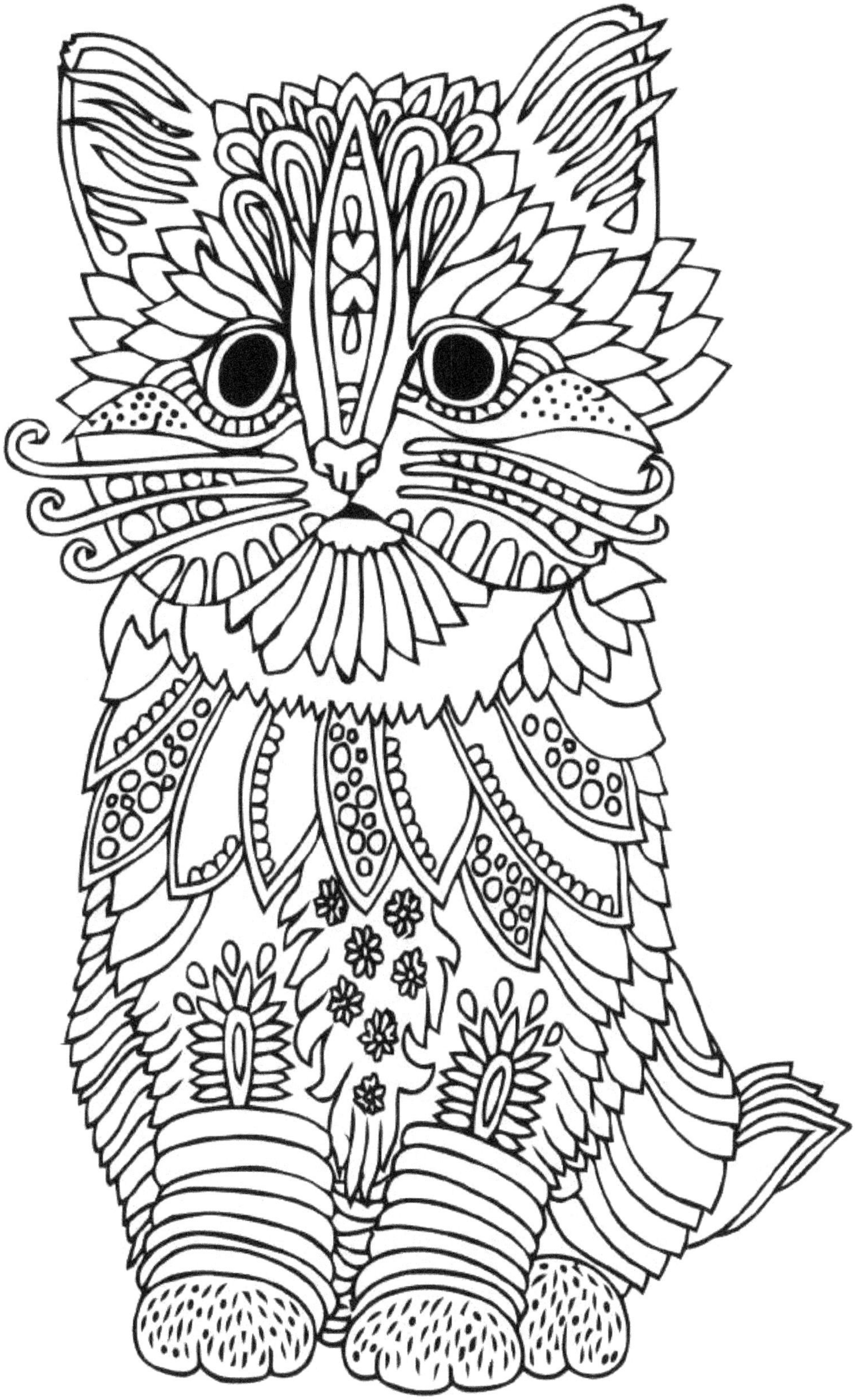

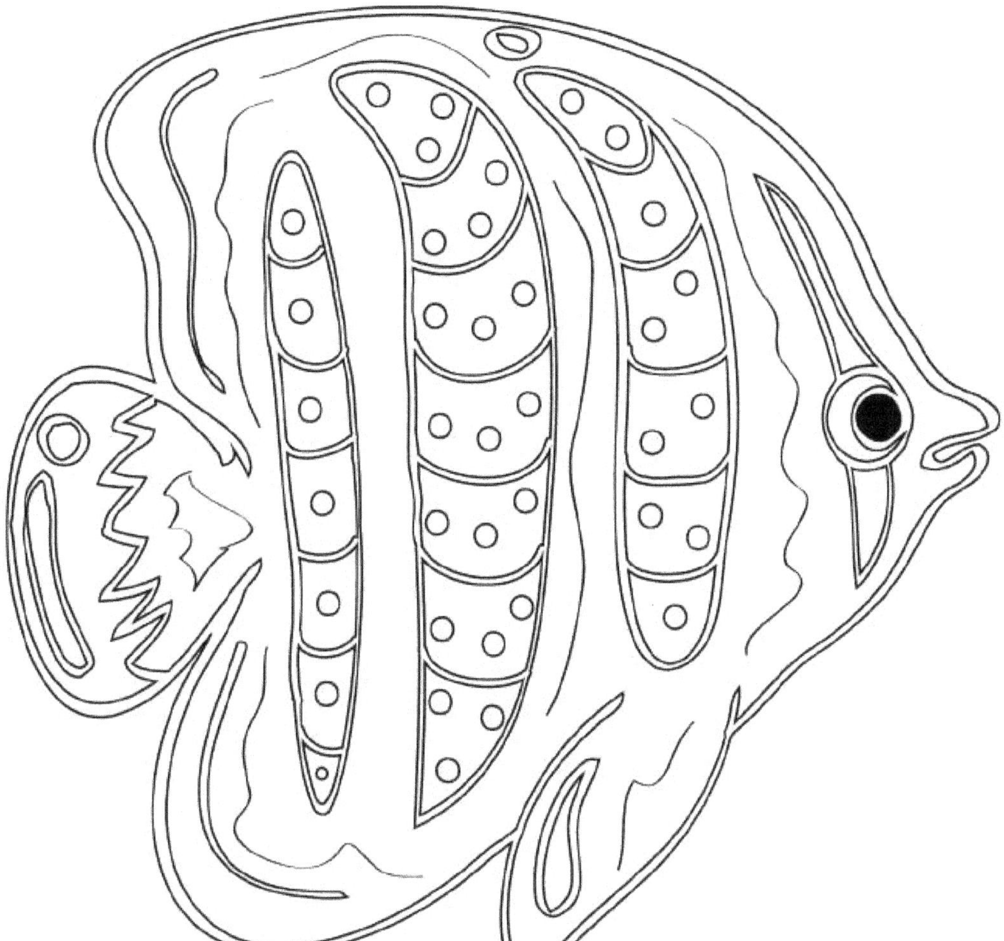

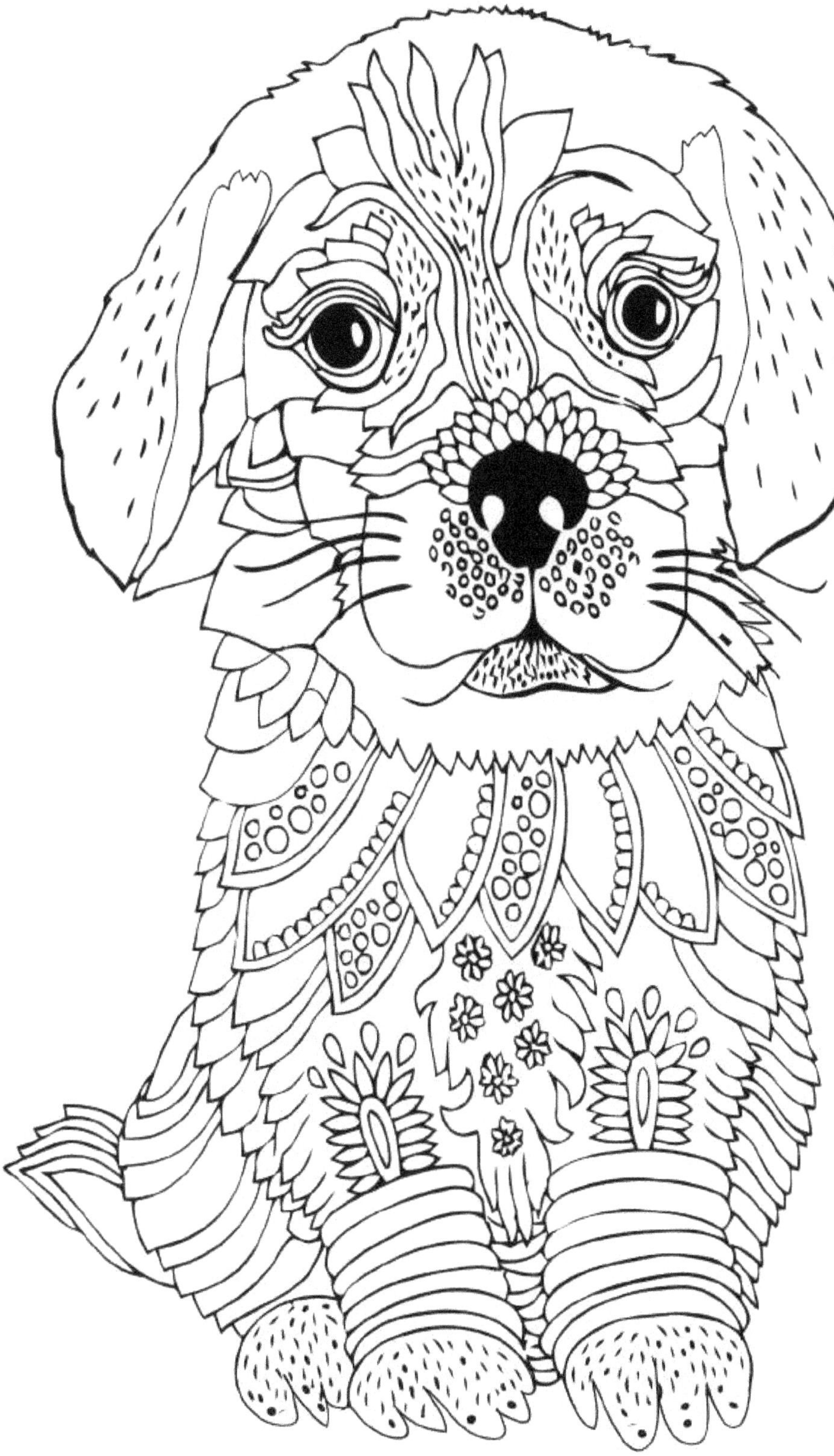

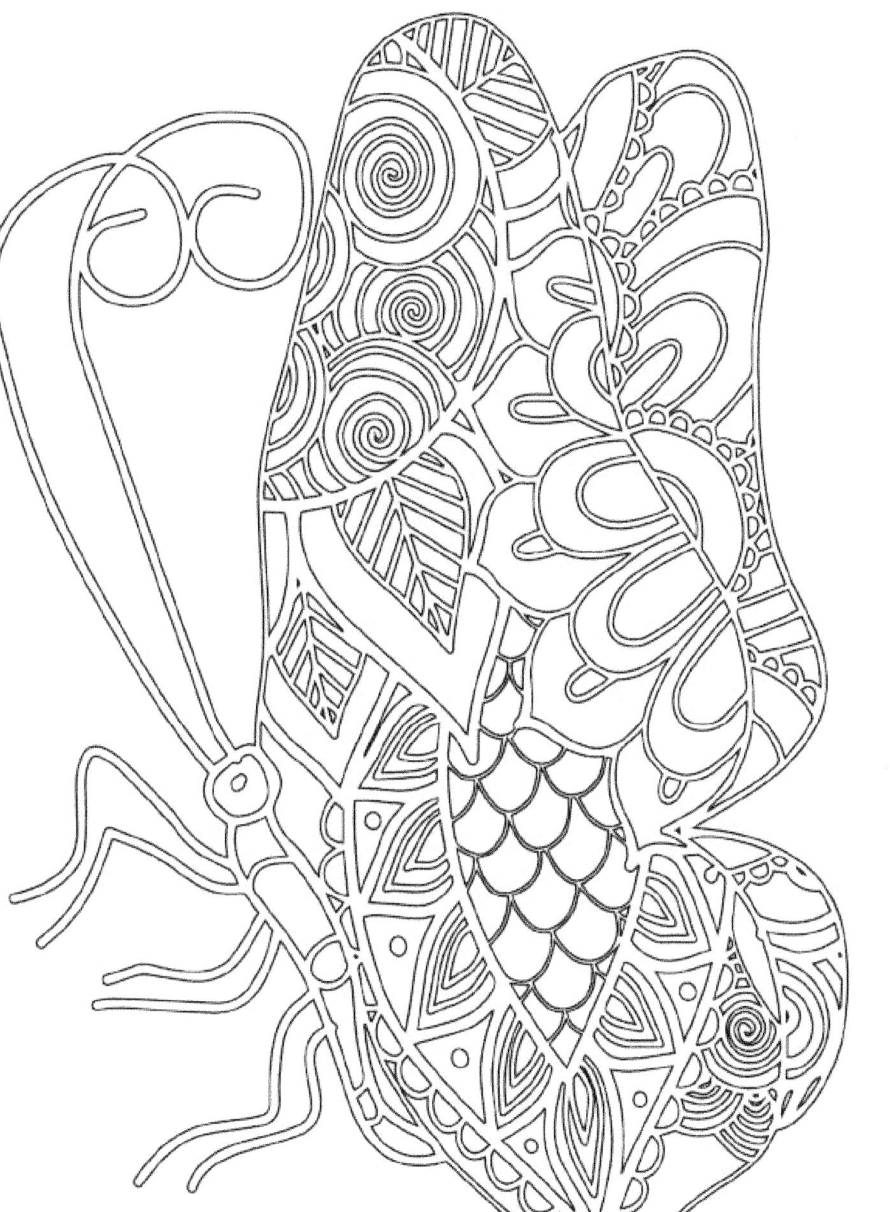

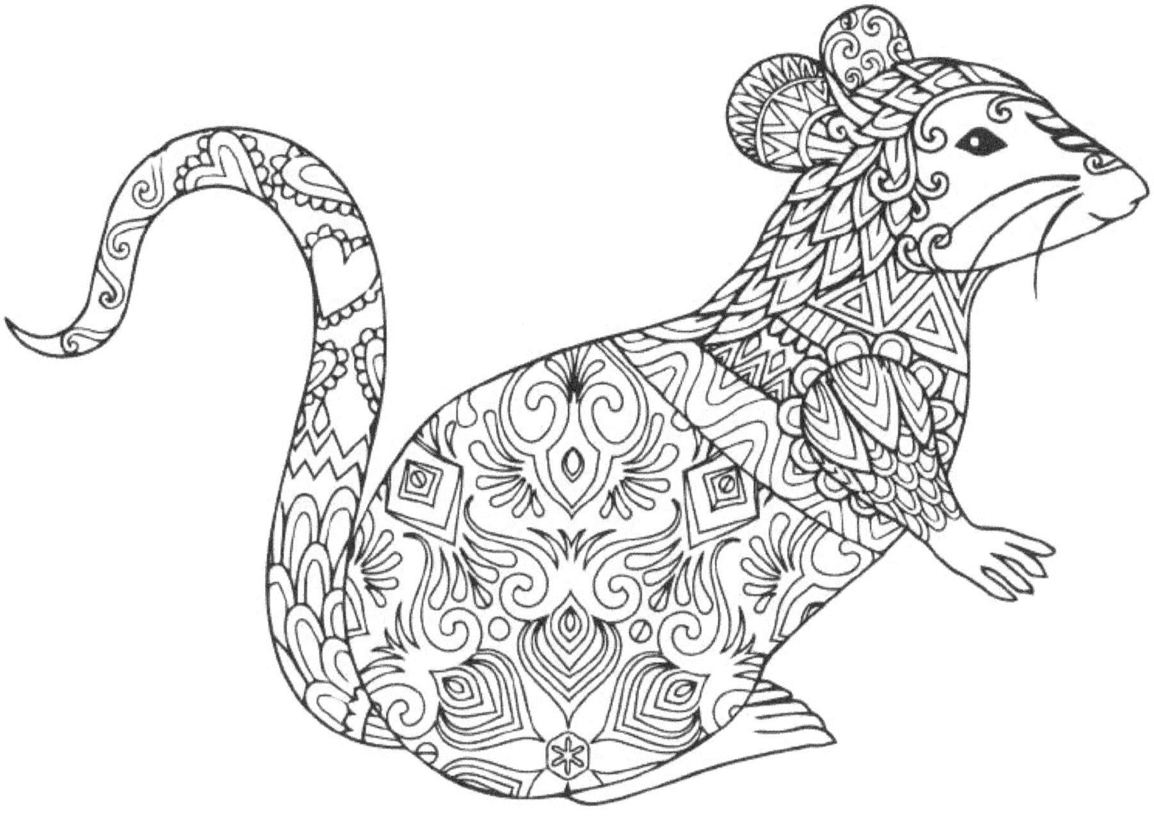

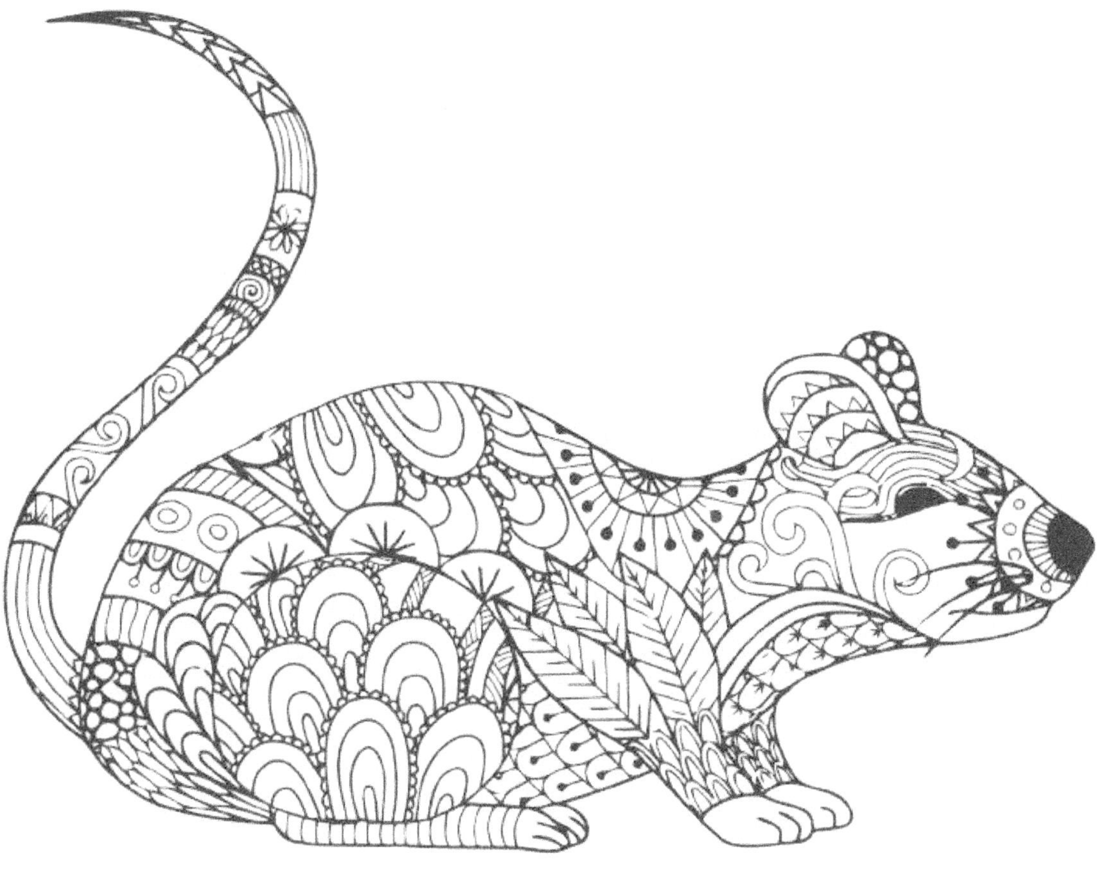

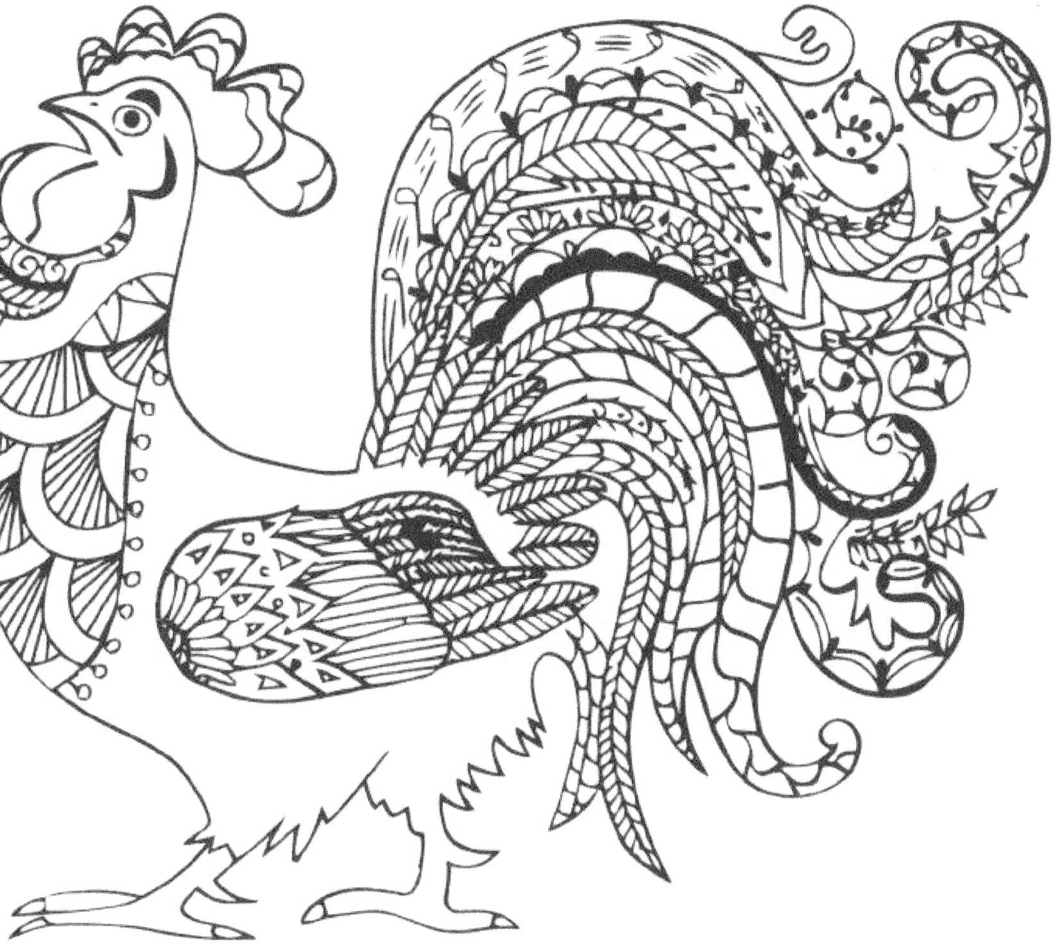

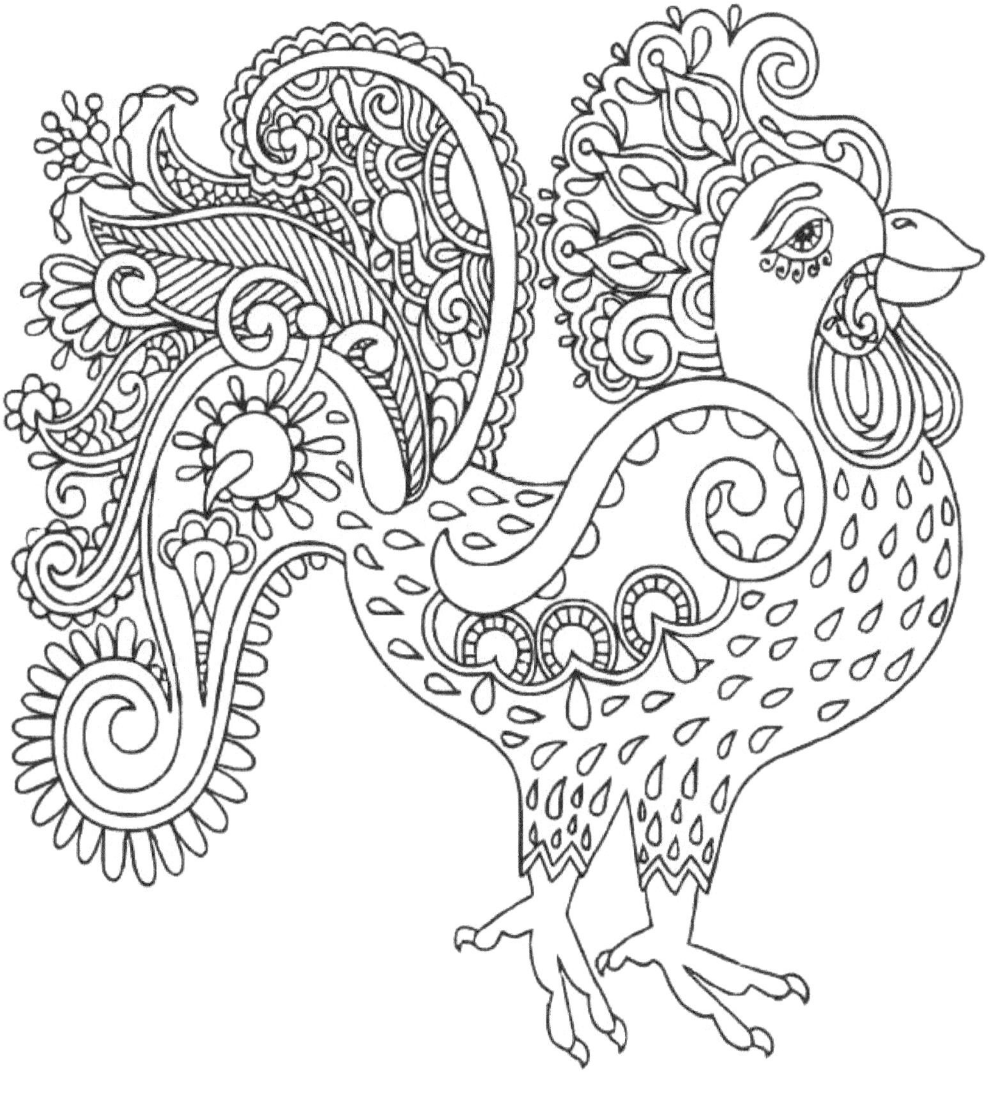

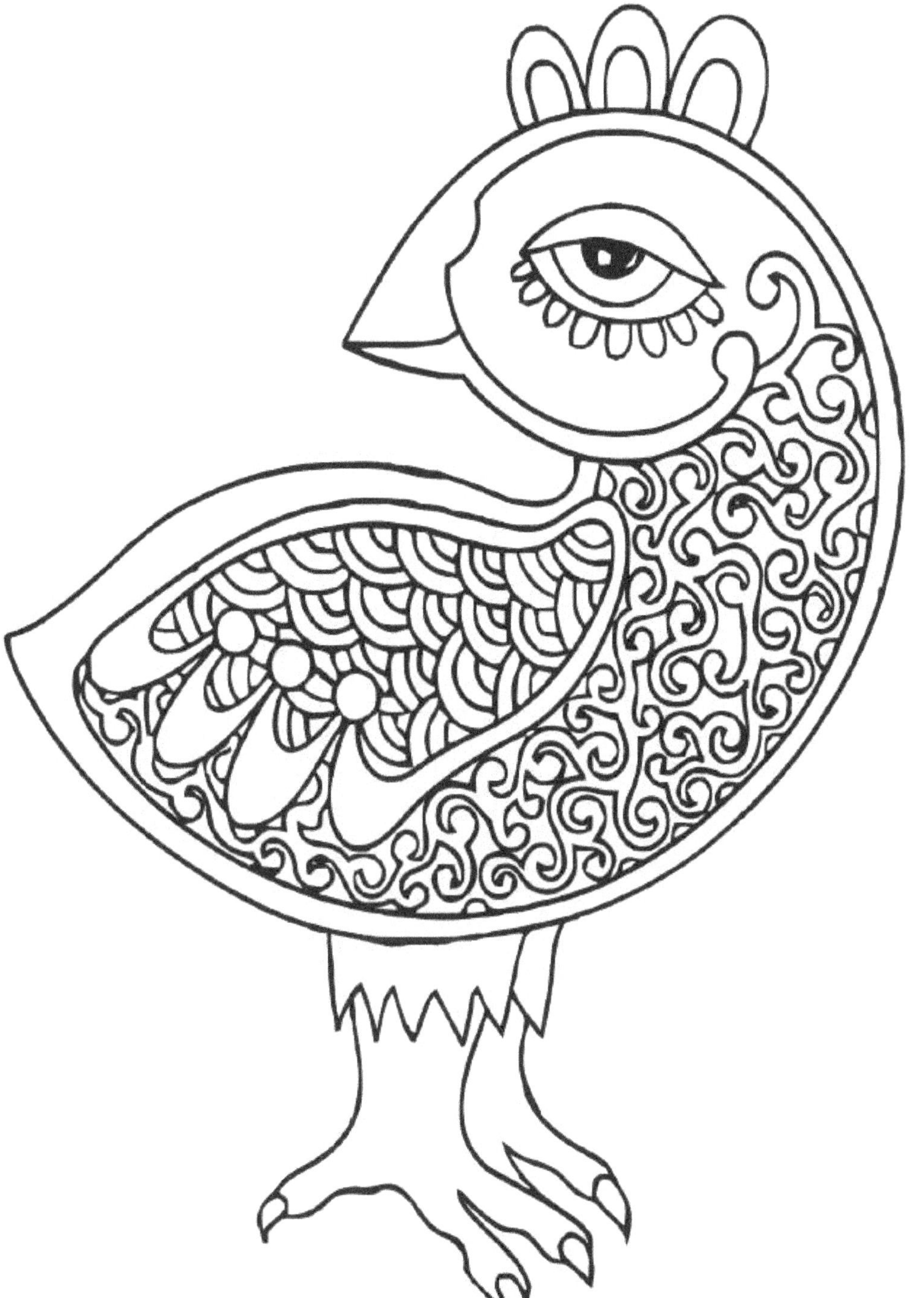

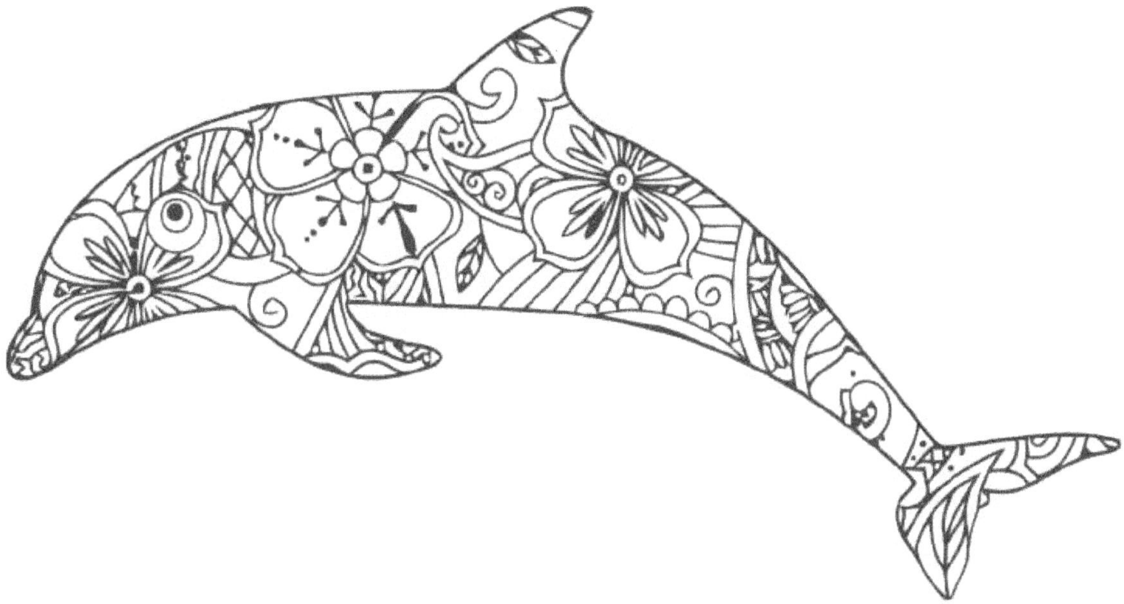

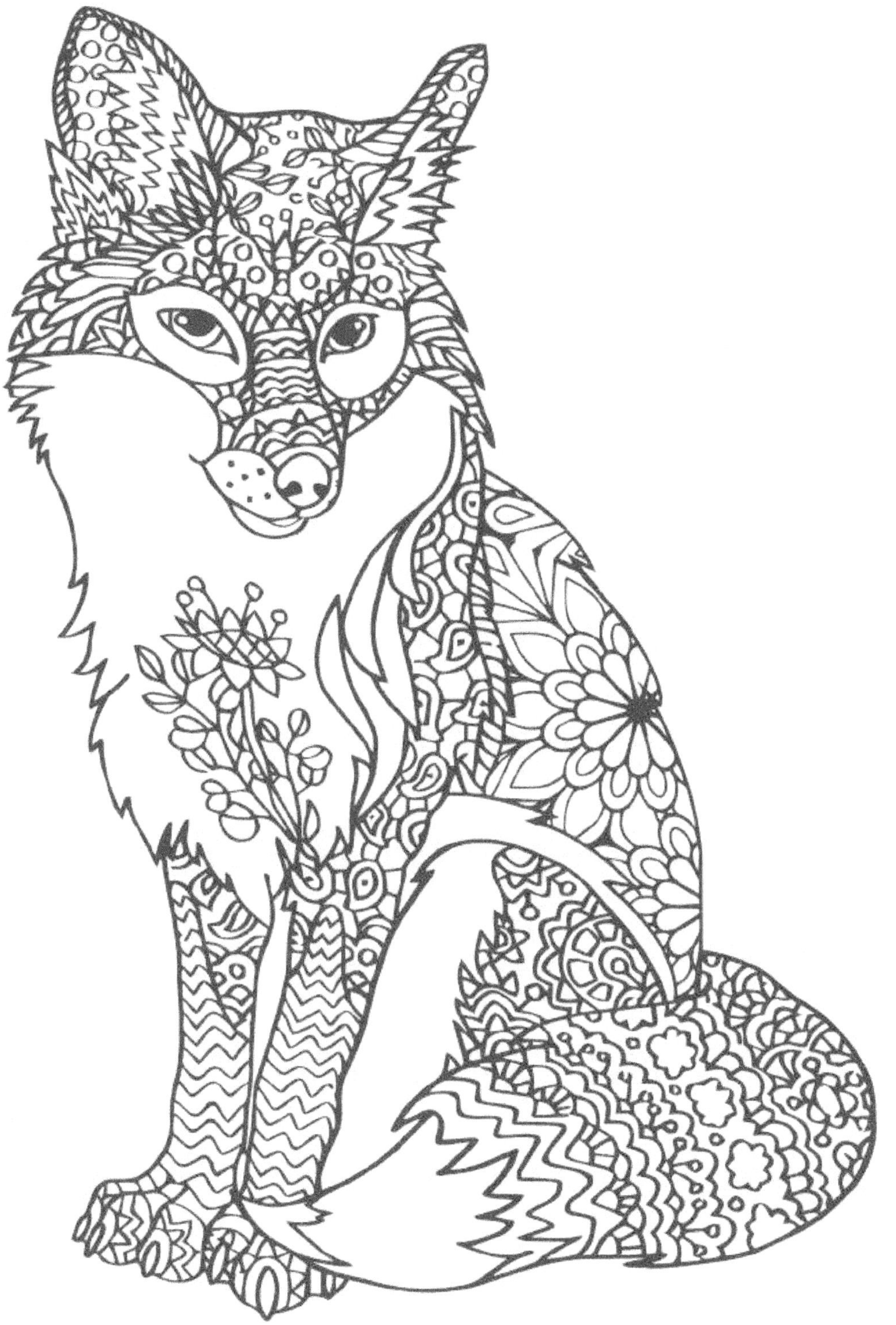

Lightning Source UK Ltd.
Milton Keynes UK
UKHW051058310521
384676UK00009B/616

9 787985 072956